vegetarian

This is a Star Fire book
First Published in 2005

06 08 09 07 05

1 3 5 7 9 10 8 6 4 2

Star Fire is part of The Foundry Creative Media Company Limited
Crabtree Hall, Crabtree Lane, Fulham, London, SW6 6TY
Please visit the our website: www.star-fire.co.uk

Please visit our cookery website: www.practicalrecipes.com

ISBN: 1-904041-28-0

The CIP record for this book is available from the British Library

Printed in China

ACKNOWLEDGEMENTS

Authors: Catherine Atkinson, Juliet Barker, Liz Martin,
Gina Steer, Carol Tennant, Mari Mereid Williams,
Elizabeth Wolf-Cohen, Simone Wright

Editorial Consultant: Gina Steer
Project Editor: Sarah Goulding

Editors: Karen Fitzpatrick, Vicky Garrard, Julia Rolf
Photography: Colin Bowling and Paul Forrester

Home Economists and Stylists: Jacqueline Bellefontaine,
Mandy Phipps, Vicki Smallwood and Penny Stephens

Design Team: Lucy Bradbury and Chris Herbert

All props supplied by Barbara Stewart at Surfaces

NOTE

Recipes using uncooked eggs should be avoided by infants, the
elderly, pregnant women and anyone suffering from an illness.

simple, straightforward recipes

vegetarian

Contents

Vitamins and Minerals

MINERALS

CALCIUM Important for healthy bones and teeth, nerve transmission, muscle contraction, blood clotting and hormone function. Calcium promotes a healthy heart, relieves aching muscles and bones and maintains the correct acid–alkaline balance. Good sources are dairy products, fish, nuts, pulses, fortified white flours, breads and green leafy vegetables.

CHROMIUM Part of the glucose tolerance factor, chromium balances blood sugar levels, helps to normalise hunger and reduce cravings, helps protect DNA and is essential for heart function. Good sources are brewer's yeast, wholemeal bread, rye bread, oysters, potatoes, green peppers, butter and parsnips.

IODINE Important for the manufacture of thyroid hormones and for normal development. Good sources of iodine are seafood, seaweed, milk and dairy products.

IRON As a component of haemoglobin, iron carries oxygen around the body. It is vital for normal growth and development. Good sources are liver, corned beef, red meat, fortified breakfast cereals, pulses, green leafy vegetables, egg yolk, cocoa and cocoa products.

MAGNESIUM Important for efficient functioning of metabolic enzymes and development of the skeleton. Magnesium promotes healthy muscles by helping them to relax and is therefore good for PMS. It is also important for heart muscles and the nervous system. Good sources are nuts, green vegetables, meat, cereals, milk and yogurt.

PHOSPHORUS Forms and maintains bones and teeth, builds muscle tissue, helps maintain pH of the body, aids metabolism and energy production. Phosphorus is present in almost all foods.

POTASSIUM Enables nutrients to move into cells, while waste products move out; promotes healthy nerves and muscles; maintains fluid balance in the body; helps secretion of insulin for blood sugar control to produce constant energy; relaxes muscles; maintains heart functioning; and stimulates gut movement to encourage proper elimination. Good sources are fruit, vegetables, milk and bread.

SELENIUM Antioxidant properties help to protect against free radicals and carcinogens. Selenium reduces inflammation, stimulates the immune system to fight infections, promotes a healthy heart and helps the action of vitamin E. It is also required for the male reproductive system and is needed for metabolism. Good sources are tuna, liver, kidney, meat, eggs, cereals, nuts and dairy products.

SODIUM Important in moderation to help control body fluid and balance. Involved in muscle and nerve function, sodium helps move nutrients into cells. All foods are good sources, but processed, pickled and salted foods are richest in sodium.

ZINC Important for metabolism and the healing of wounds. It also aids ability to cope with stress, promotes a healthy nervous system and brain, especially in the growing foetus, aids bones and teeth formation and is essential for constant energy. Good sources are liver, meat, pulses, whole-grain cereals, nuts and oysters.

VITAMINS

BIOTIN Important for metabolism of fatty acids. Good sources of biotin are liver, kidney, eggs and nuts. Micro-organisms also manufacture this vitamin in the gut.

VITAMIN A Important for cell growth and for the formation of visual pigments in the eye. Vitamin A comes in two forms: retinol and beta-carotenes. Retinol is found in liver, meat and meat products and whole milk and its products. Beta-carotene is found in red and yellow fruits and vegetables such as carrots, mangoes and apricots.

VITAMIN B1 Important in releasing energy from carboydrate-containing foods. Good sources are yeast and yeast products, bread, fortified breakfast cereals and potatoes.

VITAMIN B2 Important for the metabolism of proteins, fats and carbohydrates to produce energy. Good sources are meat, yeast extracts, fortified breakfast cereals and milk and its products.

VITAMIN B3 Required for the metabolism of food. Good sources are milk and milk products, fortified breakfast cereals, pulses, meat, poultry and eggs.

VITAMIN B5 Important for the metabolism of food and energy production. All foods are good sources but especially fortified breakfast cereals, whole-grain bread and dairy products.

VITAMIN B6 Important for the metabolism of protein and fat. Vitamin B6 may also be involved with the regulation of sex hormones. Good sources are liver, fish, pork, soya beans and peanuts.

VITAMIN B12 Important for the production of red blood cells and DNA. It is vital for growth and the nervous system. Good sources are meat, fish, eggs, poultry and milk.

VITAMIN C Important for healing wounds and forming collagen to keep skin and bones strong. It is an important antioxidant. Good sources are fruits, especially soft summer fruits and vegetables.

VITAMIN D Important for the absorption and handling of calcium to help build bone strength. Good sources are oily fish, eggs, whole milk and milk products, margarine and sufficient exposure to sunlight, as vitamin D is made in the skin.

VITAMIN E Important as an antioxidant vitamin helping to protect cell membranes from damage. Good sources are vegetable oils, margarines, seeds, nuts and green vegetables.

VITAMIN K Important for controlling blood clotting. Good sources are cauliflower, Brussels sprouts, lettuce, cabbage, beans, broccoli, peas, asparagus, potatoes, corn oil, tomatoes and milk.

Aduki Bean & Rice Burgers

Ingredients
Serves 4

2½ tbsp sunflower oil
1 medium onion,
  peeled and very
  finely chopped
1 garlic clove, peeled
  and crushed
1 tsp curry paste
225 g/8 oz uncooked
  basmati rice
400 g can aduki beans,
  drained and rinsed
225 ml/8 fl oz
  vegetable stock
125 g/4 oz firm
  tofu, crumbled
1 tsp garam masala
2 tbsp freshly
  chopped coriander
salt and freshly ground
  black pepper

For the carrot raita:

2 large carrots, peeled
  and grated
½ cucumber, cut
  into tiny cubes
150 ml/¼ pint
  Greek yogurt

To serve:

wholemeal baps
tomato slices
lettuce leaves

1 Heat 1 tablespoon of the oil in a saucepan and gently cook the onion for 10 minutes until soft. Add the garlic and curry paste and cook for a few more seconds. Stir in the rice and beans.

2 Pour in the stock, bring to the boil and simmer for 12 minutes, or until all the stock has been absorbed – do not lift the lid for the first 10 minutes of cooking. Reserve.

3 Lightly mash the tofu. Add to the rice mixture with the garam masala, coriander, salt and pepper. Mix.

4 Divide the mixture into eight and shape into burgers. Chill in the refrigerator for 30 minutes.

5 Meanwhile, make the raita. Mix together the carrots, cucumber and Greek yogurt. Spoon into a small bowl and chill in the refrigerator until ready to serve.

6 Heat the remaining oil in a large frying pan. Fry the burgers, in batches if necessary, for 4–5 minutes on each side, or until lightly browned. Serve in the baps with tomato slices and lettuce. Accompany with the raita.

Bean & Cashew Stir Fry

Ingredients

Serves 4

3 tbsp sunflower oil
1 onion, peeled and
finely chopped
1 celery stalk, trimmed
and chopped
2.5 cm/1 inch piece
fresh root ginger,
peeled and grated
2 garlic cloves, peeled
and crushed
1 red chilli, deseeded
and finely chopped
175 g/6 oz fine French
beans, trimmed
and halved
175 g/6 oz mangetout,
sliced diagonally
into 3
75 g/3 oz unsalted
cashew nuts
1 tsp brown sugar
125 ml/4 fl oz
vegetable stock
2 tbsp dry sherry
1 tbsp light soy sauce
1 tsp red wine vinegar
salt and freshly ground
black pepper
freshly chopped
coriander, to garnish

CHEF'S TIP
If you can get Chinese rice
wine, or *shaoxing*, use this
instead of the dry sherry.

1 Heat a wok or large frying pan, add the oil and when hot, add the onion and celery and stir-fry gently for 3–4 minutes or until softened.

2 Add the ginger, garlic and chilli to the wok and stir-fry for 30 seconds. Stir in the French beans and mangetout together with the cashew nuts and continue to stir-fry for 1–2 minutes, or until the nuts are golden brown.

3 Dissolve the sugar in the stock, then blend with the sherry, soy sauce and vinegar. Stir into the bean mixture and bring to the boil. Simmer gently, stirring occasionally for 3–4 minutes, or until the beans and mangetout are tender but still crisp and the sauce has thickened slightly.

4 Season to taste with salt and pepper. Transfer to a warmed serving bowl or spoon on to individual plates. Sprinkle with freshly chopped coriander and serve immediately.

Black Bean Chilli with Avocado Salsa

Ingredients
Serves 4

250 g/9 oz each of
   black beans and
   black-eye beans,
   soaked overnight
2 tbsp olive oil
1 large onion, peeled
   and finely chopped
1 red pepper, deseeded
   and diced
2 garlic cloves, peeled
   and finely chopped
1 red chilli, deseeded
   and finely chopped
2 tsp chilli powder
1 tsp ground cumin
2 tsp ground coriander
400 g can chopped
   tomatoes
450 ml/¾ pint
   vegetable stock
1 small ripe
   avocado, diced
½ small red onion, peeled
   and finely chopped
2 tbsp freshly
   chopped coriander
juice of 1 lime
1 small tomato, peeled,
   deseeded and diced
salt and black pepper
25 g/1 oz dark chocolate

To garnish:

half-fat crème fraîche
lime slices
sprigs of coriander

1 Drain the beans and place in a large saucepan with at least twice their volume of fresh water.

2 Bring slowly to the boil, skimming off any froth that rises to the surface. Boil rapidly for 10 minutes, then reduce the heat and simmer for about 45 minutes, adding more water if necessary. Drain and reserve.

3 Heat the oil in a large saucepan and add the onion and pepper. Cook for 3–4 minutes until softened. Add the garlic and chilli. Cook for 5 minutes, or until the onion and pepper have softened. Add the chilli powder, cumin and coriander and cook for 30 seconds. Add the beans along with the tomatoes and stock.

4 Bring to the boil and simmer uncovered for 40–45 minutes until the beans and vegetables are tender and the sauce has reduced.

5 Mix together the avocado, onion, fresh coriander, lime juice and tomato. Season with salt and pepper and set aside. Remove the chilli from the heat. Break the chocolate into pieces. Sprinkle over the chilli. Leave for 2 minutes. Stir well. Garnish with crème fraîche, lime and coriander. Serve with the avocado salsa.

Boston-style Baked Beans

Ingredients
Serves 8

350 g/12 oz mixed dried
   pulses, e.g. haricot,
   flageolet, cannellini,
   chickpeas or pinto
   beans
1 large onion, peeled
   and finely chopped
125 g/4 oz black treacle
   or molasses
2 tbsp Dijon mustard
2 tbsp light brown
   soft sugar
125 g/4 oz plain flour
150 g/5 oz
   fine cornmeal
2 tbsp caster sugar
2½ tsp baking powder
½ tsp salt
2 tbsp freshly
   chopped thyme
2 medium eggs
200 ml/7 fl oz milk
2 tbsp melted butter
salt and freshly ground
   black pepper
parsley sprigs,
   to garnish

1 Preheat the oven to 130°C/250°F/Gas Mark ½. Put the pulses into a large saucepan and cover with at least twice their volume of water. Bring to the boil and simmer for 2 minutes. Leave to stand for 1 hour. Return to the boil and boil rapidly for about 10 minutes. Drain and reserve.

2 Mix together the onion, treacle or molasses, mustard and sugar in a large mixing bowl. Add the drained beans and 300 ml/½ pint fresh water. Stir well, bring to the boil, cover and transfer to the preheated oven for 4 hours in an ovenproof dish, stirring once every hour and adding more water if necessary.

3 When the beans are cooked, remove from the oven and keep warm. Increase the oven temperature to 200°C/400°F/Gas Mark 6. Mix together the plain flour, cornmeal, caster sugar, baking powder, salt and most of the thyme, reserving about one third for garnish. In a separate bowl beat the eggs, then stir in the milk and butter. Pour the wet ingredients on to the dry ones and stir just enough to combine.

4 Pour into a buttered 18 cm/7 inch square cake tin. Sprinkle over the remaining thyme. Bake for 30 minutes until golden and risen or until a toothpick inserted into the centre comes out clean. Cut into squares, then reheat the beans. Season to taste with salt and pepper and serve immediately, garnished with parsley sprigs.

Bruschetta with Pecorino, Garlic & Tomatoes

Ingredients
Serves 4

6 ripe but
 firm tomatoes
125 g/4 oz pecorino
 cheese, finely grated
1 tbsp oregano leaves
salt and freshly ground
 black pepper
3 tbsp olive oil
3 garlic cloves, peeled
8 slices of flat Italian
 bread, such as focaccia
50 g/2 oz mozzarella
 cheese
marinated black olives,
 to serve

1 Preheat the grill and line the grill rack with tinfoil just before cooking. Make a small cross in the top of the tomatoes, then place in a small bowl and cover with boiling water. Leave to stand for 2 minutes, then drain and remove the skins. Cut into quarters, remove the seeds, and chop the flesh into small dice.

2 Mix the tomato flesh with the pecorino cheese and 2 teaspoons of the fresh oregano and season to taste with salt and pepper. Add 1 tablespoon of the olive oil and mix thoroughly.

3 Crush the garlic and spread evenly over the slices of bread. Heat 2 tablespoons of the olive oil in a large frying pan and sauté the bread slices until they are crisp and golden.

4 Place the fried bread on a lightly oiled baking tray and spoon on the tomato and cheese topping. Place a little mozzarella on top and place under the preheated grill for 3–4 minutes, until golden and bubbling. Garnish with the remaining oregano, then arrange the bruschettas on a serving plate and serve immediately with the olives.

CHEF'S TIP
Bitter leaves are excellent with these bruschettas. Try a mixture of frisée, radicchio and rocket. If these are unavailable, use a bag of mixed salad leaves.

Carrot & Ginger Soup

Ingredients
Serves 4

4 slices of bread,
  crusts removed
1 tsp yeast extract
2 tsp olive oil
1 onion, peeled
  and chopped
1 garlic clove, peeled
  and crushed
½ tsp ground ginger
450 g/1 lb carrots,
  peeled and chopped
1 litre/1¾ pint
  vegetable stock
2.5 cm/1 inch piece of
  root ginger, peeled
  and finely grated
salt and freshly ground
  black pepper
1 tbsp lemon juice

To garnish:

chives
lemon zest

CHEF'S TIP
Serve with a spoonful of lightly whipped or sour cream, for a special occasion.

1 Preheat the oven to 180°C/350°F/Gas Mark 4. Roughly chop the bread. Dissolve the yeast extract in 2 tablespoons of warm water and mix with the bread.

2 Spread the bread cubes over a lightly oiled baking tray and bake for 20 minutes, turning half way through. Remove from the oven and reserve.

3 Heat the oil in a large saucepan. Gently cook the onion and garlic for 3–4 minutes.

4 Stir in the ground ginger and cook for 1 minute to release the flavour.

5 Add the chopped carrots, then stir in the stock and the fresh ginger. Simmer gently for 15 minutes.

6 Remove from the heat and allow to cool a little. Blend until smooth, then season to taste with salt and pepper. Stir in the lemon juice. Garnish with the chives and lemon zest and serve immediately.

great!

Chargrilled Vegetable & Goats' Cheese Pizza

Ingredients
Serves 4

125 g/4 oz baking potato
1 tbsp olive oil
225 g/8 oz strong
   white flour
½ tsp salt
1 tsp easy-blend
   dried yeast

For the topping:

1 medium aubergine,
   thinly sliced
2 small courgettes,
   trimmed and
   sliced lengthways
1 yellow pepper,
   quartered
   and deseeded
1 red onion, peeled
   and sliced into very
   thin wedges
5 tbsp olive oil
175 g/6 oz cooked new
   potatoes, halved
400 g can chopped
   tomatoes, drained
2 tsp freshly
   chopped oregano
125 g/4 oz mozzarella
   cheese, cut into
   small cubes
125 g/4 oz goats'
   cheese, crumbled

1 Preheat the oven to 220°C/425°F/Gas Mark 7, 15 minutes before baking. Put a baking sheet in the oven to heat up. Cook the potato in lightly salted boiling water until tender. Peel and mash with the olive oil until smooth.

2 Sift the flour and salt into a bowl. Stir in the yeast. Add the mashed potato and 150 ml/¼ pint warm water and mix to a soft dough. Knead for 5–6 minutes, until smooth. Put the dough in a bowl, cover with clingfilm and leave to rise in a warm place for 30 minutes.

3 To make the topping, arrange the aubergine, courgettes, pepper and onion, skin-side up, on a grill rack and brush with 4 tablespoons of the oil. Grill for 4–5 minutes. Turn the vegetables and brush with the remaining oil. Grill for 3–4 minutes. Cool, skin and slice the pepper. Put all of the vegetables in a bowl, add the halved new potatoes and toss gently together. Set aside.

4 Briefly re-knead the dough then roll out to a 30.5–35.5 cm/ 12–14 inch round, according to preferred thickness. Mix the tomatoes and oregano together and spread over the pizza base. Scatter over the mozzarella cheese. Put the pizza on the preheated baking sheet and bake for 8 minutes.

5 Arrange the vegetables and goats' cheese on top and bake for 8–10 minutes. Serve.

Cheese & Onion Oat Pie

Bit dry - Oats hard to toast. Use a less oats! potatoes not quite cooked

Ingredients

Serves 4

1 tbsp sunflower oil, plus 1 tsp
25 g/1 oz butter
2 medium onions, peeled and sliced
1 garlic clove, peeled and crushed
150 g/5 oz porridge oats
125 g/4 oz mature Cheddar cheese, grated
2 medium eggs, lightly beaten
2 tbsp freshly chopped parsley
salt and freshly ground black pepper
275 g/10 oz baking potato, peeled

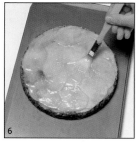

1 Preheat the oven to 180°C/350°F/Gas Mark 4. Heat the oil and half the butter in a saucepan until melted. Add the onions and garlic and gently cook for 10 minutes, or until soft. Remove from the heat and tip into a large bowl.

2 Spread the oats out on a baking sheet and toast in the hot oven for 12 minutes. Leave to cool, then add to the onions with the cheese, eggs and parsley. Season to taste with salt and pepper and mix well.

3 Line the base of a 20.5 cm/8 inch round sandwich tin with greaseproof paper and oil well. Thinly slice the potato and arrange the slices on the base, overlapping them slightly.

4 Spoon the cheese and oat mixture on top of the potato, spreading evenly with the back of a spoon. Cover with tinfoil and bake for 30 minutes.

5 Invert the pie onto a baking sheet so that the potatoes are on top. Carefully remove the tin and lining paper.

6 Preheat the grill to medium. Melt the remaining butter and carefully brush over the potato topping. Cook under the preheated grill for 5–6 minutes until the potatoes are lightly browned. Cut into wedges and serve.

Chinese Salad with Soy & Ginger Dressing

Ingredients
Serves 4

1 head of
   Chinese cabbage
200 g can water
   chestnuts, drained
6 spring
   onions, trimmed
4 ripe but firm
   cherry tomatoes
125 g/4 oz mangetout
125 g/4 oz beansprouts
2 tbsp freshly
   chopped coriander

For the soy and ginger dressing:

2 tbsp sunflower oil
4 tbsp light soy sauce
2.5 cm/1 inch piece root
   ginger, peeled and
   finely grated
zest and juice of
   1 lemon
salt and freshly ground
   black pepper
crusty white bread,
   to serve

CHEF'S TIP
Sprinkling the tomatoes with a small amount of sugar will draw out the bitter juices, and add an intensity to the flavour. Be sure to drain off the juices before serving.

1 Rinse and finely shred the Chinese cabbage and place in a serving dish.

2 Slice the water chestnuts into small slivers and cut the spring onions diagonally into 2.5 cm/1 inch lengths, then split lengthwise into thin strips.

3 Cut the tomatoes in half and then slice each half into three wedges and reserve.

4 Simmer the mangetout in boiling water for 2 minutes until beginning to soften, drain and cut in half diagonally.

5 Arrange the water chestnuts, spring onions, mangetout, tomatoes and beansprouts on top of the shredded Chinese cabbage. Garnish with the freshly chopped coriander.

6 Make the dressing by whisking all the ingredients together in a small bowl until mixed thoroughly. Serve with the bread and the salad.

Chunky Vegetable & Fennel Goulash with Dumplings

Ingredients
Serves 4

2 fennel bulbs,
  weighing about
  450 g/1 lb
2 tbsp sunflower oil
1 large onion, peeled
  and sliced
1½ tbsp paprika
1 tbsp plain flour
300 ml/½ pint
  vegetable stock
400 g can chopped
  tomatoes
450 g/1 lb potatoes,
  peeled and cut into
  2.5 cm/1 inch chunks
125 g/4 oz small
  button mushrooms
salt and freshly ground
  black pepper

For the dumplings:

1 tbsp sunflower oil
1 small onion, peeled
  and finely chopped
1 medium egg
3 tbsp milk
3 tbsp freshly
  chopped parsley
125 g/4 oz fresh white
  breadcrumbs

1 Cut the fennel bulbs in half widthways. Thickly slice the stalks and cut the bulbs into eight wedges. Heat the oil in a large saucepan or flameproof casserole dish. Add the onion and fennel and cook gently for 10 minutes until soft. Stir in the paprika and flour.

2 Remove from the heat and gradually stir in the stock. Add the chopped tomatoes, potatoes and mushrooms. Season to taste with salt and pepper. Bring to the boil, reduce the heat and simmer for 20 minutes.

3 Meanwhile, make the dumplings. Heat the oil in a frying pan and gently cook the onion for 10 minutes, until soft. Leave to cool for a few minutes.

4 In a bowl, beat the egg and milk together, then add the onion, parsley and breadcrumbs and season to taste. With damp hands form the breadcrumb mixture into 12 round dumplings each about the size of a walnut.

5 Arrange the dumplings on top of the goulash. Cover and cook for a further 15 minutes until the dumplings are cooked and the vegetables are tender. Serve immediately.

Courgette & Tarragon Tortilla

Ingredients
Serves 6

700 g/1½ lb potatoes
3 tbsp olive oil
1 onion, peeled and
    thinly sliced
salt and freshly ground
    black pepper
1 courgette, trimmed
    and thinly sliced
6 medium eggs
2 tbsp freshly
    chopped tarragon
tomato wedges,
    to serve

1 Peel the potatoes and thinly slice. Dry the slices in a clean tea towel to get them as dry as possible. Heat the oil in a large, heavy-based pan, add the onion and cook for 3 minutes. Add the potatoes with a little salt and pepper, then stir the potatoes and onion gently to coat in the oil.

2 Reduce the heat to the lowest possible setting, cover and cook gently for 5 minutes. Turn the potatoes and onion over and continue to cook for a further 5 minutes. Give the pan a shake every now and again to ensure that the potatoes do not stick to the base or burn. Add the courgette, then cover and cook for a further 10 minutes.

3 Beat the eggs and tarragon together and season to taste with salt and pepper. Pour the egg mixture over the vegetables and return to the heat. Cook on a low heat for up to 20–25 minutes, or until there is no liquid egg left on the surface of the tortilla.

4 Turn the tortilla over by inverting the tortilla onto the lid or onto a flat plate. Return the pan to the heat and cook for a final 3–5 minutes, or until the underside is golden brown. If preferred, place the tortilla under a preheated grill for 4 minutes, or until set and golden brown on top. Cut into small squares and serve hot or cold with tomato wedges.

Italian Baked Tomatoes with Curly Endive & Radicchio

Ingredients
Serves 4

1 tsp olive oil
4 beef tomatoes
salt
50 g/2 oz fresh
   white breadcrumbs
1 tbsp freshly
   snipped chives
1 tbsp freshly
   chopped parsley
125 g/4 oz button
   mushrooms,
   finely chopped
salt and freshly ground
   black pepper
25 g/1 oz fresh parmesan
   cheese, grated

For the salad:

½ curly endive lettuce
½ small piece
   of radicchio
2 tbsp olive oil
1 tsp balsamic vinegar
salt and freshly ground
   black pepper

CHEF'S TIP
As an alternative, try stirring in 2 tablespoons of either tapenade or ready-made pesto into the stuffing mixture. Alternatively, replace the chives with freshly chopped basil.

1 Preheat the oven to 190°C/375°F/Gas Mark 5. Lightly oil a baking tray with the teaspoon of oil. Slice the tops off the tomatoes, remove all the tomato flesh and sieve into a large bowl. Sprinkle a little salt inside the tomato shells and then place them upside down on a plate while the filling is prepared.

2 Mix the sieved tomato with the breadcrumbs, fresh herbs and mushrooms and season well with salt and pepper. Place the tomato shells on the prepared baking tray and fill with the tomato and mushroom mixture. Sprinkle the cheese on the top and bake in the preheated oven for 15–20 minutes, until golden brown.

3 Meanwhile, prepare the salad. Arrange the endive and radicchio on individual serving plates and mix the remaining ingredients together in a small bowl to make the dressing. Season to taste.

4 When the tomatoes are cooked, allow to rest for 5 minutes, then place on the prepared plates and drizzle over a little dressing. Serve warm.

Bit dry. Use fresh bread? very fresh. Milk?

Layered Cheese & Herb Potato Cake

Ingredients
Serves 4

900 g/2 lb waxy potatoes
3 tbsp freshly snipped chives
2 tbsp freshly chopped parsley
225 g/8 oz mature Cheddar cheese
2 large egg yolks
1 tsp paprika
125 g/4 oz fresh white breadcrumbs
50 g/2 oz almonds, toasted and roughly chopped
50 g/2 oz butter, melted
salt and freshly ground black pepper
mixed salad or steamed vegetables, to serve

1 Preheat the oven to 180°C/350°F/Gas Mark 4. Lightly oil and line the base of a 20.5 cm/8 inch round cake tin with lightly oiled greaseproof or baking parchment paper. Peel and thinly slice the potatoes and reserve. Stir the chives, parsley, cheese and egg yolks together in a small bowl and reserve. Mix the paprika into the breadcrumbs.

2 Sprinkle the almonds over the base of the lined tin. Cover with half the potatoes, arranging them in layers, then sprinkle with the paprika breadcrumb mixture and season to taste with salt and pepper.

3 Spoon the cheese and herb mixture over the breadcrumbs with a little more seasoning, then arrange the remaining potatoes on top. Drizzle over the melted butter and press the surface down firmly.

4 Bake in the preheated oven for 1¼ hours, or until golden and cooked through. Let the tin stand for 10 minutes before carefully turning out and serving in thick wedges. Serve immediately with salad or freshly cooked vegetables.

CHEF'S TIP
If the potatoes still feel a little hard when poked with a skewer but the top is well-browned, cover the cake with tinfoil for the rest of the cooking time.

Leek & Potato Tart

Ingredients
Serves 6

225 g/8 oz plain flour
pinch of salt
150 g/5 oz butter, cubed
50 g/2 oz walnuts, very
    finely chopped
1 large egg yolk

For the filling:

450 g/1 lb leeks,
    trimmed and
    thinly sliced
40 g/1½ oz butter
450 g/1 lb large new
    potatoes, scrubbed
300 ml/½ pint
    soured cream
3 medium eggs,
    lightly beaten
175 g/6 oz Gruyère
    cheese, grated
freshly grated nutmeg
salt and freshly ground
    black pepper
fresh chives, to garnish

CHEF'S TIP
To vary the crust, try
replacing the walnuts
with other kinds of nut, or
replace the nuts with
3 tablespoons of freshly
chopped, mixed herbs.

1 Preheat the oven to 200°C/400°F/Gas Mark 6, about 15 minutes before baking. Sift the flour and salt into a bowl. Rub in the butter until the mixture resembles breadcrumbs. Stir in the nuts. Mix together the egg yolk and 3 tablespoons of cold water. Sprinkle over the dry ingredients. Mix to form a dough.

2 Knead on a lightly floured surface for a few seconds, then wrap in clingfilm and chill in the refrigerator for 20 minutes. Roll out and use to line a 20.5 cm/8 inch spring-form tin or very deep flan tin. Chill for a further 30 minutes.

3 Cook the leeks in the butter over a high heat for 2–3 minutes, stirring constantly. Lower the heat, cover and cook for 25 minutes until soft, stirring occasionally. Remove the leeks from the heat.

4 Cook the potatoes in boiling salted water for 15 minutes, or until almost tender. Drain and thickly slice. Add to the leeks. Stir the soured cream into the leeks and potatoes, followed by the eggs, cheese, nutmeg and salt and pepper. Pour into the pastry case and bake on the middle shelf in the preheated oven for 20 minutes.

5 Reduce the oven temperature to 190°C/375°F/Gas Mark 5 and cook for a further 30–35 minutes, or until the filling is set. Garnish with chives and serve immediately.

Light Ratatouille

Ingredients
Serves 4

1 red pepper
2 courgettes, trimmed
1 small aubergine, trimmed
1 onion, peeled
2 ripe tomatoes
50 g/2 oz button mushrooms, wiped and halved or quartered
200 ml/7 fl oz tomato juice
1 tbsp freshly chopped basil
salt and freshly ground black pepper

1 Deseed the peppers, remove the membrane with a small sharp knife and cut into small dice. Thickly slice the courgettes and cut the aubergine into small dice. Slice the onion into rings.

2 Place the tomatoes in boiling water until their skins begin to peel away.

3 Remove the skins from the tomatoes, cut into quarters and remove the seeds.

4 Place all the vegetables in a saucepan with the tomato juice and basil. Season to taste with salt and pepper.

5 Bring to the boil, cover and simmer for 15 minutes or until the vegetables are tender.

6 Remove the vegetables with a slotted spoon and arrange in a serving dish.

7 Bring the liquid in the pan to the boil and boil for 20 seconds until it is slightly thickened. Season the sauce to taste with salt and pepper.

8 Pass the sauce through a sieve to remove some of the seeds and pour over the vegetables. Serve the ratatouille hot or cold.

Mediterranean Potato Salad

Ingredients
Serves 4

700 g/1½ lb small
   waxy potatoes
2 red onions, peeled
   and roughly chopped
1 yellow pepper,
   deseeded and
   roughly chopped
1 green pepper,
   deseeded and
   roughly chopped
6 tbsp extra virgin
   olive oil
125 g/4 oz ripe
   tomatoes, chopped
50 g/2 oz pitted black
   olives, sliced
125 g/4 oz feta cheese
3 tbsp freshly
   chopped parsley
2 tbsp white
   wine vinegar
1 tsp Dijon mustard
1 tsp clear honey
salt and freshly ground
   black pepper
sprigs of fresh parsley,
   to garnish

CHEF'S TIP
When buying tomatoes,
look for ones sold still
attached to the vine for a
particularly rich flavour.

1 Preheat the oven to 200°C/400°F/Gas Mark 6. Place the potatoes in a large saucepan of salted water, bring to the boil and simmer until just tender. Do not overcook. Drain and plunge into cold water, to stop them from cooking further.

2 Place the onions in a bowl with the yellow and green peppers, then pour over 2 tablespoons of the olive oil. Stir and spoon onto a large baking tray. Cook in the preheated oven for 25–30 minutes, or until the vegetables are tender and lightly charred in places, stirring occasionally. Remove from the oven and transfer to a large bowl.

3 Cut the potatoes into bite-sized pieces and mix with the roasted onions and peppers. Add the tomatoes and olives to the potatoes. Crumble over the feta cheese and sprinkle with the chopped parsley.

4 Whisk together the remaining olive oil, vinegar, mustard and honey, then season to taste with salt and pepper. Pour the dressing over the potatoes and toss gently together. Garnish with parsley sprigs and serve immediately.

Mixed Grain Pilaf

Ingredients

Serves 4

2 tbsp olive oil
1 garlic clove, peeled
    and crushed
½ tsp ground turmeric
125 g/4 oz mixed long-
    grain and wild rice
50 g/2 oz red lentils
300 ml/½ pint
    vegetable stock
200 g can chopped
    tomatoes
5 cm/2 inch piece
    cinnamon stick
salt and freshly ground
    black pepper
400 g can mixed beans,
    drained and rinsed
15 g/½ oz butter
1 bunch spring
    onions, trimmed
    and finely sliced
3 medium eggs
4 tbsp freshly chopped
    herbs, such as parsley
    and chervil
sprigs of fresh dill,
    to garnish

1 Heat 1 tablespoon of the oil in a saucepan. Add the garlic and turmeric and cook for a few seconds. Stir in the rice and lentils.

2 Add the stock, tomatoes and cinnamon. Season to taste with salt and pepper. Stir once and bring to the boil. Lower the heat, cover and simmer for 20 minutes, until most of the stock is absorbed and the rice and lentils are tender.

3 Stir in the beans, replace the lid and leave to stand for 2–3 minutes to allow the beans to heat through.

4 While the rice is cooking, heat the remaining oil and butter in a frying pan. Add the spring onions and cook for 4–5 minutes, until soft. Lightly beat the eggs with 2 tablespoons of the herbs, then season with salt and pepper.

5 Pour the egg mixture over the spring onions. Stir gently with a spatula over a low heat, drawing the mixture from the sides to the centre as the omelette sets. When almost set, stop stirring and cook for about 30 seconds until golden underneath.

6 Remove the omelette from the pan, roll up and slice into thin strips. Fluff the rice up with a fork and remove the cinnamon stick. Spoon onto serving plates, top with strips of omelette and the remaining chopped herbs. Garnish with sprigs of dill and serve.

Mixed Vegetable Stir Fry

Ingredients
Serves 4

2 tbsp groundnut oil
4 garlic cloves, peeled
   and finely sliced
2.5 cm/1 inch piece fresh
   root ginger, peeled
   and finely sliced
75 g/3 oz broccoli florets
50 g/2 oz mangetout,
   trimmed
75 g/3 oz carrots,
   peeled and cut
   into matchsticks
1 green pepper, deseeded
   and cut into strips
1 red pepper, deseeded
   and cut into strips
1 tbsp soy sauce
1 tbsp hoisin sauce
1 tsp sugar
salt and freshly ground
   black pepper
4 spring onions,
   trimmed and
   shredded, to garnish

1 Heat a wok, add the oil and when hot, add the garlic and ginger slices and stir-fry for 1 minute.

2 Add the broccoli florets to the wok, stir-fry for 1 minute, then add the mangetout, carrots and the green and red peppers and stir-fry for a further 3–4 minutes, or until tender but still crisp.

3 Blend the soy sauce, hoisin sauce and sugar in a small bowl. Stir well, season to taste with salt and pepper and pour into the wok.

4 Transfer the vegetables to a warmed serving dish. Garnish with shredded spring onions and serve immediately.

CHEF'S TIP
Vary the combination of vegetables – try asparagus spears cut into short lengths, sliced mushrooms, French beans, red onion wedges and cauliflower florets.

Mushroom Stew

Ingredients
Serves 4

15 g/½ oz dried
   porcini mushrooms
900 g/2 lb assorted
   fresh mushrooms,
   wiped
2 tbsp good quality
   virgin olive oil
1 onion, peeled and
   finely chopped
2 garlic cloves, peeled
   and finely chopped
1 tbsp fresh
   thyme leaves
pinch of ground cloves
salt and freshly ground
   black pepper
700 g/1½ lb tomatoes,
   peeled, deseeded
   and chopped
225 g/8 oz
   instant polenta
600ml/1 pint
   vegetable stock
3 tbsp freshly chopped
   mixed herbs
sprigs of parsley,
   to garnish

CHEF'S TIP

For a richer version of this recipe, add a generous splash of red wine in step 5, and enrich with 2 tablespoons of sour cream before serving.

1 Soak the porcini mushrooms in a small bowl of hot water for 20 minutes.

2 Drain, reserving the porcini mushrooms and their soaking liquor. Cut the fresh mushrooms in half and reserve.

3 In a saucepan, heat the oil and add the onion.

4 Cook gently for 5–7 minutes until softened. Add the garlic, thyme and cloves and continue cooking for 2 minutes.

5 Add all the mushrooms and cook for 8–10 minutes until the mushrooms have softened, stirring often. Season to taste with salt and pepper and add the tomatoes and the reserved soaking liquor.

6 Simmer, partly covered, over a low heat for about 20 minutes until thickened. Adjust the seasoning to taste.

7 Meanwhile, cook the polenta according to the packet instructions using the vegetable stock. Stir in the herbs and divide between four dishes.

8 Ladle the mushrooms over the polenta, garnish with the parsley and serve immediately.

Peperonata

Ingredients
Serves 6

2 red peppers
2 yellow peppers
450 g/1 lb waxy
  potatoes
1 large onion
2 tbsp good quality
  virgin olive oil
700 g/1½ lb tomatoes,
  peeled, deseeded
  and chopped
2 small courgettes
50 g/2 oz pitted black
  olives, quartered
small handful
  basil leaves
salt and freshly ground
  black pepper
crusty bread, to serve

1 Prepare the peppers by halving them lengthwise and removing the stems, seeds, and membranes.

2 Cut the peppers lengthwise into strips about 1 cm/½ inch wide. Peel the potatoes and cut into rough cubes, about 2.5–3 cm/1–1¼ inch across. Cut the onion lengthwise into eight wedges.

3 Heat the olive oil in a large saucepan over a medium heat.

4 Add the onion and cook for about 5 minutes, or until starting to brown.

5 Add the peppers, potatoes, tomatoes, courgettes, black olives and about four torn basil leaves. Season to taste with salt and pepper.

6 Stir the mixture, cover and cook over a very low heat for about 40 minutes, or until the vegetables are tender but still hold their shape. Garnish with the remaining basil. Transfer to a serving bowl and serve immediately, with chunks of crusty bread.

CHEF'S TIP
Chunks of baguette, as shown in the picture, would work well with this recipe but you could also use freshly baked ciabatta or foccacia, which would add an extra taste of the Mediterranean.

Potato Gnocchi with Pesto Sauce

Ingredients
Serves 6

900 g/2 lb floury
    potatoes
40 g/1½ oz butter
1 medium egg, beaten
225 g/8 oz plain flour
1 tsp salt
freshly ground
    black pepper
25 g/1 oz Parmesan
    cheese, shaved
rocket salad, to serve

For the
pesto sauce:

50 g/2 oz fresh
    basil leaves
1 large garlic
    clove, peeled
2 tbsp pine nuts
125 ml/4 fl oz olive oil
40 g/1½ oz Parmesan
    cheese, grated

1 Cook the potatoes in their skins in boiling water for 20 minutes, or until tender. Drain and peel. While still warm, push the potatoes through a fine sieve into a bowl. Stir in the butter, egg, 175 g/6 oz of the flour, the salt and pepper.

2 Sift the remaining flour onto a board or work surface, add the potato mixture. Gently knead in enough flour until a soft, slightly sticky dough is formed.

3 With floured hands, break off portions of the dough and roll into 2.5 cm/1 inch thick ropes. Cut into 2 cm/¾ inch lengths. Lightly press each piece against the inner prongs of a fork. Put on a tray covered with a floured tea towel and chill in the refrigerator for about 30 minutes.

4 To make the pesto sauce, place the basil, garlic, pine nuts and oil in a processor and blend until smooth and creamy. Turn into a bowl and stir in the Parmesan cheese. Season to taste.

5 Cooking in several batches, drop the gnocchi into a saucepan of barely simmering salted water. Cook for 3–4 minutes, or until they float to the surface. Remove with a slotted spoon and keep warm in a covered oiled baking dish in a low oven.

6 Add the gnocchi to the pesto sauce and toss gently to coat. Serve immediately, scattered with the Parmesan cheese and accompanied by a rocket salad.

Red Lentil Kedgeree with Avocado & Tomatoes

Ingredients
Serves 4

150 g/5 oz basmati rice
150 g/5 oz red lentils
15 g/½ oz butter
1 tbsp sunflower oil
1 medium onion, peeled
   and chopped
1 tsp ground cumin
4 cardamom
   pods, bruised
1 bay leaf
450 ml/¾ pint
   vegetable stock
1 ripe avocado, peeled,
   stoned and diced
1 tbsp lemon juice
4 plum tomatoes,
   peeled and diced
2 tbsp freshly
   chopped coriander
salt and freshly ground
   black pepper
lemon or lime slices,
   to garnish

1 Put the rice and lentils into a sieve and rinse under cold running water. Tip into a bowl, then pour over enough cold water to cover and leave to soak for 10 minutes.

2 Heat the butter and oil in a saucepan. Add the sliced onion and cook gently, stirring occasionally, for 10 minutes until softened. Stir in the cumin, cardamom pods and bay leaf and cook for a further minute, stirring all the time.

3 Drain the rice and lentils, rinse again and add to the onions in the saucepan. Stir in the vegetable stock and bring to the boil. Reduce the heat, cover the saucepan and simmer for 14–15 minutes, or until the rice and lentils are tender.

4 Place the diced avocado in a bowl and toss with the lemon juice. Stir in the tomatoes and chopped coriander. Season to taste with salt and pepper.

5 Fluff up the rice with a fork, spoon into a warmed serving dish and spoon the avocado mixture on top. Garnish with lemon or lime slices and serve.

Sicilian Baked Aubergine

Ingredients
Serves 4

1 large aubergine,
   trimmed
2 celery stalks, trimmed
4 large ripe tomatoes
1 tsp sunflower oil
2 shallots, peeled and
   finely chopped
1½ tsp tomato purée
25 g/1 oz green
   pitted olives
25 g/1 oz black
   pitted olives
salt and freshly ground
   black pepper
1 tbsp white
   wine vinegar
2 tsp caster sugar
1 tbsp freshly chopped
   basil, to garnish
mixed salad leaves,
   to serve

1 Preheat the oven to 200°C/400°F/Gas Mark 6. Cut the aubergine into small cubes and place on an oiled baking tray.

2 Cover the tray with tinfoil and bake in the preheated oven for 15–20 minutes until soft. Reserve, to allow the aubergine to cool.

3 Place the celery and tomatoes in a large bowl and cover with boiling water.

4 Remove the tomatoes from the bowl when their skins begin to peel away. Remove the skins then deseed and chop the flesh into small pieces.

5 Remove the celery from the bowl of water, finely chop and reserve.

6 Pour the vegetable oil into a non-stick saucepan, add the chopped shallots and fry gently for 2–3 minutes until soft. Add the celery, tomatoes, tomato purée and olives. Season to taste with salt and pepper.

7 Simmer gently for 3–4 minutes. Add the vinegar, sugar and cooled aubergine to the pan and heat gently for 2–3 minutes until all the ingredients are well blended. Reserve to allow the aubergine mixture to cool. When cool, garnish with the chopped basil and serve cold with salad leaves.

Spiced Couscous & Vegetables

Ingredients
Serves 4

1 tbsp olive oil
1 large shallot, peeled
    and finely chopped
1 garlic clove, peeled
    and finely chopped
1 small red pepper,
    deseeded and cut
    into strips
1 small yellow pepper,
    deseeded and cut
    into strips
1 small aubergine, diced
1 tsp each turmeric,
    ground cumin,
    ground cinnamon
    and paprika
2 tsp ground coriander
large pinch
    saffron strands
2 tomatoes, peeled,
    deseeded and diced
2 tbsp lemon juice
225 g/8 oz couscous
225 ml/8 fl oz
    vegetable stock
2 tbsp raisins
2 tbsp whole almonds
2 tbsp freshly
    chopped parsley
2 tbsp freshly
    chopped coriander
salt and freshly ground
    black pepper

1 Heat the oil in a large frying pan and add the shallot and garlic and cook for 2–3 minutes until softened. Add the peppers and aubergine and reduce the heat.

2 Cook for 8–10 minutes until the vegetables are tender, adding a little water if necessary.

3 Test a piece of aubergine to ensure it is cooked through. Add all the spices and cook for a further minute, stirring.

4 Increase the heat and add the tomatoes and lemon juice. Cook for 2–3 minutes until the tomatoes have started to break down. Remove from the heat and leave to cool slightly.

5 Meanwhile, put the couscous into a large bowl. Bring the stock to the boil in a saucepan, then pour over the couscous. Stir well and cover with a clean tea towel.

6 Leave to stand for 7–8 minutes until all the stock is absorbed and the couscous is tender.

7 Uncover the couscous and fluff with a fork. Stir in the vegetable and spice mixture along with the raisins, almonds, parsley and coriander. Season to taste with salt and pepper and serve.

Spinach Dumplings with Rich Tomato Sauce

Ingredients
Serves 4

For the sauce

2 tbsp olive oil
1 onion, peeled
   and chopped
1 garlic clove, peeled
   and crushed
1 red chilli, deseeded
   and chopped
150 ml/¼ pint dry
   white wine
400 g can chopped
   tomatoes
pared strip of
   lemon rind

For the dumplings:

450 g/1 lb fresh spinach
50 g/2 oz ricotta cheese
25 g/1 oz fresh white
   breadcrumbs
25 g/1 oz parmesan
   cheese, grated
1 medium egg yolk
¼ tsp freshly
   grated nutmeg
salt and freshly ground
   black pepper
5 tbsp plain flour
2 tbsp olive oil, for frying
fresh basil leaves,
   to garnish
freshly cooked
   tagliatelle, to serve

1 To make the tomato sauce, heat the olive oil in a large saucepan and fry the onion gently for 5 minutes. Add the garlic and chilli and cook for a further 5 minutes, until softened.

2 Stir in the wine, chopped tomatoes and lemon rind. Bring to the boil, cover and simmer for 20 minutes, then uncover and simmer for 15 minutes, or until the sauce has thickened. Remove the lemon rind and season to taste with salt and pepper.

3 To make the spinach dumplings, wash the spinach thoroughly and remove any tough stalks. Cover and cook in a large saucepan over a low heat with just the water clinging to the leaves. Drain, then squeeze out all the excess water. Finely chop and put in a large bowl.

4 Add the ricotta, breadcrumbs, parmesan cheese and egg yolk to the spinach. Season with nutmeg and salt and pepper. Mix together and shape into 20 walnut-sized balls.

5 Toss the spinach balls in the flour. Heat the olive oil in a large non-stick frying pan and fry the balls gently for 5–6 minutes, carefully turning occasionally. Garnish with fresh basil leaves and serve immediately with the tomato sauce and tagliatelle.

Swede, Turnip, Parsnip & Potato Soup

Ingredients
Serves 4

2 large onions, peeled
25 g/1 oz butter
2 medium carrots,
   peeled and
   roughly chopped
175 g/6 oz swede,
   peeled and
   roughly chopped
125 g/4 oz turnip, peeled
   and roughly chopped
125 g/4 oz parsnips,
   peeled and
   roughly chopped
175 g/6 oz
   potatoes, peeled
1 litre/1¾ pints
   vegetable stock
½ tsp freshly
   grated nutmeg
salt and freshly ground
   black pepper
4 tbsp vegetable oil,
   for frying
125 ml/4 fl oz
   double cream
warm crusty bread,
   to serve

CHEF'S TIP
For a lower-fat version of this soup use semi-skimmed milk instead of cream, when reheating.

1 Finely chop 1 onion. Melt the butter in a large saucepan and add the onion, carrots, swede, turnip, parsnip and potatoes. Cover and cook gently for about 10 minutes, without colouring. Stir occasionally during this time.

2 Add the stock and season to taste with the nutmeg, salt and pepper. Cover and bring to the boil, then reduce the heat and simmer gently for 15–20 minutes, or until the vegetables are tender. Remove from the heat and leave to cool for 30 minutes.

3 Heat the oil in a large heavy-based frying pan. Add the onions and cook over a medium heat, for about 2–3 minutes, stirring frequently, until golden brown. Remove the onions with a slotted spoon and drain well on absorbent kitchen paper. As they cool, they will turn crispy.

4 Pour the cooled soup into a food processor or blender and process to form a smooth purée. Return to the cleaned pan, adjust the seasoning, then stir in the cream. Gently reheat and top with the crispy onions. Serve immediately with chunks of bread.

Sweet Potato Cakes with Mango & Tomato Salsa

Ingredients
Serves 4

700 g/1½ lb sweet
 potatoes, peeled and
 cut into large chunks
25 g/1 oz butter
1 onion, peeled
 and chopped
1 garlic clove, peeled
 and crushed
pinch of freshly
 grated nutmeg
salt and freshly ground
 black pepper
1 medium egg, beaten
50 g/2 oz quick-cook
 polenta
2 tbsp sunflower oil

For the salsa:

1 ripe mango, peeled,
 stoned and diced
6 cherry tomatoes, cut
 in wedges
4 spring onions,
 trimmed and
 thinly sliced
1 red chilli, deseeded
 and finely chopped
finely grated rind and
 juice of ½ lime
2 tbsp freshly
 chopped mint
1 tsp clear honey
salad leaves, to serve

1 Steam or cook the sweet potatoes in lightly salted boiling water for 15–20 minutes, until tender. Drain well, then mash until smooth.

2 Melt the butter in a saucepan. Add the onion and garlic and cook gently for 10 minutes until soft. Add to the mashed sweet potato and season with the nutmeg, salt and pepper. Stir together until mixed thoroughly. Leave to cool.

3 Shape the mixture into four oval potato cakes, about 2.5 cm/1 inch thick. Dip first in the beaten egg, allowing the excess to fall back into the bowl, then coat in the polenta. Refrigerate for at least 30 minutes.

4 Meanwhile, mix together all the ingredients for the salsa. Spoon into a serving bowl, cover with clingfilm and leave at room temperature to allow the flavours to develop.

5 Heat the oil in a frying pan and cook the potato cakes for 4–5 minutes on each side. Serve with the salsa and salad leaves.

Thai Curry with Tofu

Ingredients
Serves 4

750 ml/1¼ pints
   coconut milk
700 g/1½ lb tofu,
   drained and cut
   into small cubes
salt and freshly ground
   black pepper
4 garlic cloves, peeled
   and chopped
1 large onion, peeled
   and cut into wedges
1 tsp crushed
   dried chillies
grated rind of 1 lemon
2.5 cm/1 inch piece
   fresh root ginger,
   peeled and grated
1 tbsp ground coriander
1 tsp ground cumin
1 tsp turmeric
2 tbsp light soy sauce
1 tsp cornflour
Thai fragrant rice,
   to serve

To garnish:

2 red chillies, deseeded
   and cut into rings
1 tbsp freshly
   chopped coriander
lemon wedges

CHEF'S TIP
Use firm tofu for this dish,
whether plain, marinated
or smoked, all of which are
available from health food
and Oriental shops as well
as supermarkets.

1 Pour 600 ml/1 pint of the coconut milk into a saucepan and bring to the boil. Add the tofu, season to taste with salt and pepper and simmer gently for 10 minutes. Using a slotted spoon, remove the tofu and place on a plate. Reserve the coconut milk.

2 Place the garlic, onion, dried chillies, lemon rind, ginger, spices and soy sauce into a blender or food processor and blend until a smooth paste is formed. Pour the remaining 150 ml/¼ pint coconut milk into a clean saucepan and whisk in the spicy paste. Cook, stirring continuously, for 15 minutes, or until the curry sauce is very thick.

3 Gradually whisk the reserved coconut milk into the curry and heat to simmering point. Add the cooked tofu and cook for 5–10 minutes. Blend the cornflour with 1 tablespoon of cold water and stir into the curry. Cook until thickened. Turn into a warmed serving dish and garnish with chilli, lemon wedges and coriander. Serve immediately with Thai fragrant rice.

Thai-style Cauliflower & Potato Curry

Ingredients
Serves 4

450 g/1 lb new potatoes, peeled and halved or quartered

350 g/12 oz cauliflower florets

3 garlic cloves, peeled and crushed

1 onion, peeled and finely chopped

40 g/1½ oz ground almonds

1 tsp ground coriander

½ tsp ground cumin

½ tsp turmeric

3 tbsp groundnut oil

salt and freshly ground black pepper

50 g/2 oz creamed coconut, broken into small pieces

200 ml/7 fl oz vegetable stock

1 tbsp mango chutney

sprigs of fresh coriander, to garnish

freshly cooked long-grain rice, to serve

CHEF'S TIP
Take care not to overcook the cauliflower; it should be only just tender for this dish. Broccoli florets would make a good alternative.

1 Bring a saucepan of lightly salted water to the boil, add the potatoes and cook for 15 minutes or until just tender. Drain and leave to cool. Boil the cauliflower for 2 minutes, then drain and refresh under cold running water. Drain again and reserve.

2 Meanwhile, blend the garlic, onion, ground almonds and spices with 2 tablespoons of the oil and salt and pepper to taste in a food processor until a smooth paste is formed. Heat a wok, add the remaining oil and when hot, add the spice paste and cook for 3–4 minutes, stirring continuously.

3 Dissolve the creamed coconut in 6 tablespoons of boiling water and add to the wok. Pour in the stock, cook for 2–3 minutes, then stir in the cooked potatoes and cauliflower.

4 Stir in the mango chutney and heat through for 3–4 minutes or until piping hot. Tip into a warmed serving dish, garnish with sprigs of fresh coriander and serve immediately with freshly cooked rice.

Vegetable Tempura

Ingredients
Serves 4–6

125 g/4 oz rice flour
75 g/3 oz plain flour
4 tsp baking powder
1 tbsp dried
    mustard powder
2 tsp semolina
salt and freshly ground
    black pepper
300 ml/½ pint
    groundnut oil
125 g/4 oz courgette,
    trimmed and
    thickly sliced
125 g/4 oz mangetout
125 g/4 oz baby
    sweetcorn
4 small red onions,
    peeled and quartered
1 large red pepper,
    deseeded and cut
    into 2.5 cm/1 inch
    wide strips
light soy sauce,
    to serve

1 Sift the rice flour and the plain flour into a large bowl, then sift in the baking powder and dried mustard powder.

2 Stir the semolina into the flour mixture and season to taste with salt and pepper. Gradually beat in 300 ml/½ pint cold water to produce a thin coating batter. Leave to stand at room temperature for 30 minutes.

3 Heat a wok or large frying pan, add the oil and heat to 180°C/ 350°F. Working in batches and using a slotted spoon, dip the vegetables in the batter until well coated, then drop them carefully into the hot oil. Cook each batch for 2–3 minutes or until golden. Drain on absorbent kitchen paper and keep warm while cooking the remaining batches.

4 Transfer the vegetables to a warmed serving platter and serve immediately with the light soy sauce to use as a dipping sauce.

CHEF'S TIP
When deep-frying the vegetables, only cook a few at a time, otherwise the temperature of the oil will drop and the fritters will not be crisp.

Vegetable Thai Spring Rolls

Ingredients
Serves 4

50 g/2 oz cellophane
    vermicelli
4 dried shiitake
    mushrooms
1 tbsp groundnut oil
2 medium carrots,
    peeled and cut into
    fine matchsticks
125 g/4 oz mangetout,
    cut lengthways into
    fine strips
3 spring onions,
    trimmed
    and chopped
125 g/4 oz canned
    bamboo shoots, cut
    into fine matchsticks
1 cm/½ inch piece fresh
    root ginger, peeled
    and grated
1 tbsp light soy sauce
1 medium egg,
    separated
salt and freshly ground
    black pepper
20 spring roll wrappers,
    each about 12.5 cm/
    5 inch square
vegetable oil for
    deep-frying
spring onion tassels,
    to garnish

1 Place the vermicelli in a bowl and pour over enough boiling water to cover. Leave to soak for 5 minutes or until softened, then drain. Cut into 7.5 cm/3 inch lengths. Soak the shiitake mushrooms in almost boiling water for 15 minutes, drain, discard the stalks and slice thinly.

2 Heat a wok or large frying pan, add the groundnut oil and when hot, add the carrots and stir-fry for 1 minute. Add the mangetout and spring onions and stir-fry for 2–3 minutes or until tender. Tip the vegetables into a bowl and leave to cool.

3 Stir the vermicelli and shiitake mushrooms into the cooled vegetables with the bamboo shoots, ginger, soy sauce and egg yolk. Season to taste with salt and pepper and mix thoroughly.

4 Brush the edges of a spring roll wrapper with a little beaten egg white. Spoon 2 teaspoons of the vegetable filling on to the wrapper, in a 7.5 cm/3 inch log shape 2.5 cm/1 inch from one edge. Fold the wrapper edge over the filling, then fold in the right and left sides. Brush the folded edges with more egg white and roll up neatly. Place on an oiled baking sheet, seam-side down and make the rest of the spring rolls.

5 Heat the oil in a heavy-based saucepan or deep-fat fryer to 180°C/350°F. Deep-fry the spring rolls, six at a time for 2–3 minutes, or until golden brown and crisp. Drain on absorbent kitchen paper and arrange on a warmed platter. Garnish with spring onion tassels and serve immediately.

Vegetables in Coconut Milk with Rice Noodles

Ingredients
Serves 4

75 g/3 oz creamed coconut

1 tsp salt

2 tbsp sunflower oil

2 garlic cloves, peeled and finely chopped

2 red peppers, deseeded and cut into thin strips

2.5 cm/1 inch piece of fresh root ginger, peeled and cut into thin strips

125 g/4 oz baby sweetcorn

2 tsp cornflour

2 medium ripe but still firm avocados

1 small Cos lettuce, cut into thick strips

freshly cooked rice noodles, to serve

1 Roughly chop the creamed coconut, place in a bowl with the salt, then pour over 600 ml/1 pint of boiling water. Stir until the coconut has dissolved completely and reserve.

2 Heat a wok or large frying pan, add the oil and when hot, add the chopped garlic, sliced peppers and ginger. Cook for 30 seconds, then cover and cook very gently for 10 minutes or until the peppers are soft.

3 Pour in the reserved coconut milk and bring to the boil. Stir in the baby sweetcorn, cover and simmer for 5 minutes. Blend the cornflour with 2 teaspoons of water, pour into the wok and cook, stirring, for 2 minutes or until thickened slightly.

4 Cut the avocados in half, peel, remove the stone and slice. Add to the wok with the lettuce strips and stir until well mixed and heated through. Serve immediately on a bed of rice noodles.

CHEF'S TIP
Most rice noodles need to be soaked briefly in boiling water before use, but always check the packet instructions as soaking times may vary.

Warm Noodle Salad with Sesame & Peanut Dressing

Ingredients
Serves 4–6

125 g/4 oz smooth
   peanut butter
6 tbsp sesame oil
3 tbsp light soy sauce
2 tbsp red wine vinegar
1 tbsp freshly grated
   root ginger
2 tbsp double cream
250 g pack Chinese fine
   egg noodles
125 g/4 oz beansprouts
225 g/8 oz baby
   sweetcorn
125 g/4 oz carrots,
   peeled and cut
   into matchsticks
125 g/4 oz mangetout
125 g/4 oz cucumber,
   cut into thin strips
3 spring onions,
   trimmed and
   finely shredded

CHEF'S TIP
Careful preparation will save time in this recipe. Cut the vegetables into small, uniform pieces and have everything ready before you cook.

1 Place the peanut butter, 4 tablespoons of the sesame oil, the soy sauce, vinegar and ginger in a food processor. Blend until smooth, then stir in 75 ml/3 fl oz hot water and blend again. Pour in the cream, blend briefly until smooth. Pour the dressing into a jug and reserve.

2 Bring a saucepan of lightly salted water to the boil, add the noodles and beansprouts and cook for 4 minutes or according to the packet instructions. Drain, rinse under cold running water and drain again. Stir in the remaining sesame oil and keep warm.

3 Bring a saucepan of lightly salted water to the boil and add the baby sweetcorn, carrots and mangetout and cook for 3–4 minutes, or until just tender but still crisp. Drain and cut the mangetout in half. Slice the baby sweetcorn (if very large) into 2–3 pieces and arrange on a warmed serving dish with the noodles. Add the cucumber strips and spring onions. Spoon over a little of the dressing and serve immediately with the remaining dressing.

simple, straightforward recipes **vegetarian**

Index

THE WHALE

WHO WANTED MORE

For all the souls of this Uni-verse*,
who are remembering the tune. — R B

*(One-song)

For my littlest nephew Charlie
— welcome to the world — J F

ORCHARD BOOKS

First published in Great Britain in 2021
by The Watts Publishing Group

1 3 5 7 9 10 8 6 4 2

Text © Rachel Bright, 2021
Illustrations © Jim Field, 2021

A CIP catalogue record for this book is available from the British Library.

HB ISBN 978 1 40834 923 6
PB ISBN 978 1 40834 922 9

Printed and bound in China

FSC
www.fsc.org

MIX
Paper from
responsible sources
FSC® C104740

Orchard Books, an imprint of Hachette Children's Group
Part of The Watts Publishing Group Limited
Carmelite House,
50 Victoria Embankment,
London EC4Y 0DZ
An Hachette UK Company
www.hachette.co.uk
www.hachettechildrens.co.uk

ORCHARD

Rachel
BRIGHT

Jim
FIELD

THE WHALE
WHO WANTED MORE

Under glittering waves of a vast ocean blue,
A beautiful world is hidden from view.
And there, in the cool and the quiet of the deep,
A great, gentle giant was stirring from sleep.

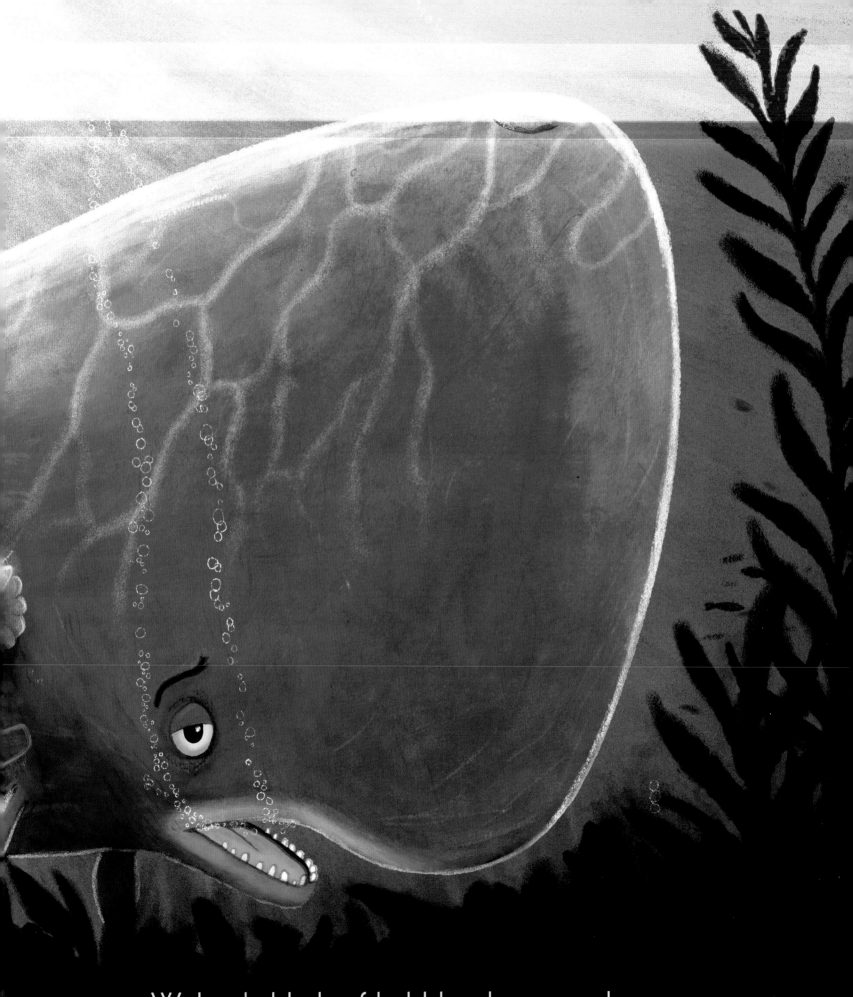

With a hubbub of bubbles, he opened one eye
And let out a long, lonely, rippling sigh.

For when Humphrey awoke, he remembered his QUEST,
One that pulled at his heart and pressed at his chest.
A life-longing search for . . . he didn't know what . . .
He just KNEW it was something he hadn't yet got!

He'd rifled in shipwrecks and rooted through treasure,

Scooped pretty shells, which
he'd polish for pleasure.

But whether his haul
was enormous or tiny . . .

. . . The next day, it just never seemed quite as **SHINY**.

So he **NEVER** felt satisfied, that was for sure,
And, no matter the bounty, he just wanted **MORE**.

BUT, the more he amassed, the more lonesome he got.
He knew it was wrong, but he just couldn't stop.

So he drifted, without any sense of direction,
Till his WONDERINGS washed him, one day . . .

...TO PERFECTION!

A rainbow of reefs
kissed with speckles of sun,
Where all kinds of critters
hung out and had fun.
There were glistening fishes,
crustaceans galore,
There were molluscs and dugongs
and urchins and more!

The coral was studded with
flotsam and jetsam.
Humphrey just wanted to
dive in and get some!

Meanwhile, on
this reef, once a
magical home,
chaos and trouble,
it bubbled and foamed.
Since with so many
creatures all crammed
in one place,
There were too many
neighbours and not
enough space.

They all **BICKERED** and **SNIPPERED**.

They **PUSHED** and they **SHOVED**.

And so did not notice . . .

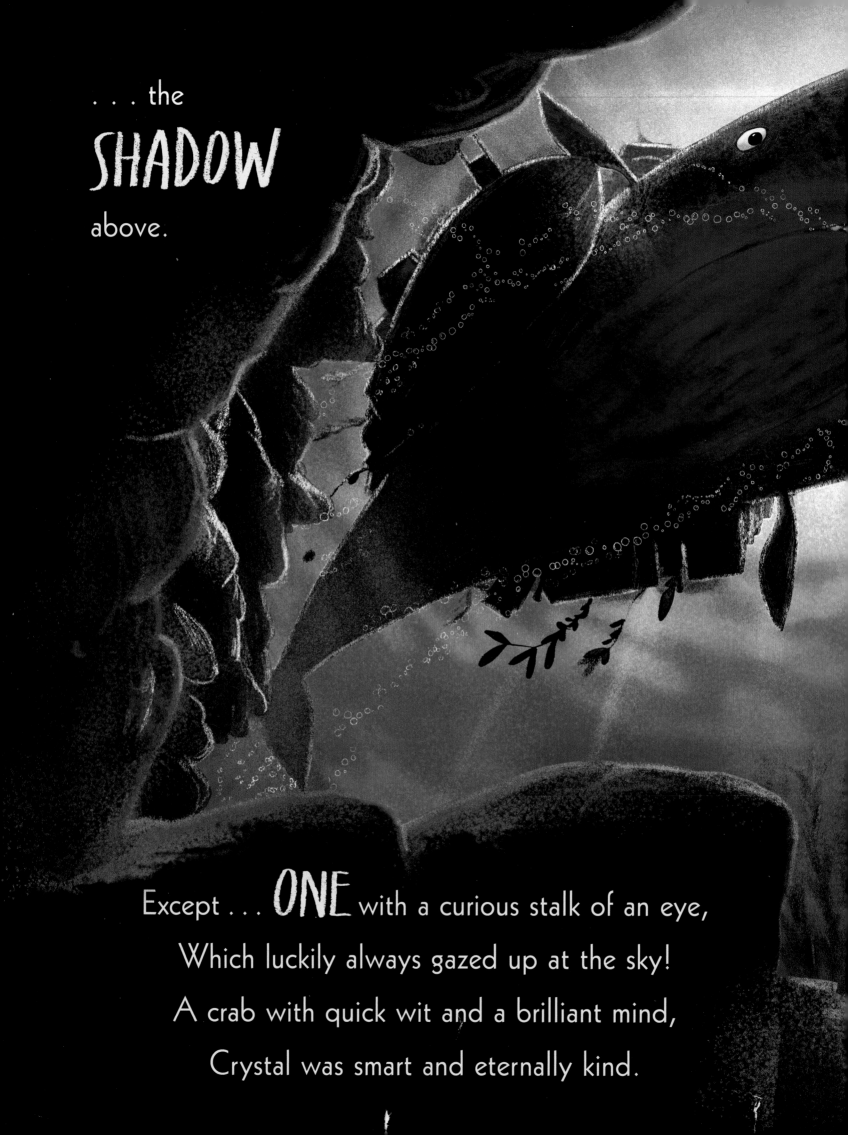

. . . the
SHADOW
above.

Except . . . **ONE** with a curious stalk of an eye,
Which luckily always gazed up at the sky!
A crab with quick wit and a brilliant mind,
Crystal was smart and eternally kind.

"LOOK UP!" Crystal shouted.
"LOOK UP AND LOOK OUT
THE WHALE WHO WANTS MORE
IS OUT AND ABOUT!"

But all were so busy
with one gripe or another,
They hadn't got time
to look out for each other.
So Humphrey, he plunged
in the noise of the brawl
to fill up his longing

ONCE AND FOR ALL!

"HELLLLLLP!" they all screamed,
gripped by panic and fear.
But, as everyone froze,
Crystal's thinking was clear . . .

"**WHALE!**"
Crystal shouted.

"**WHALE,
YOU
MUST
STOP!**"

She yelled it so loud that

she thought she might pop!

"**YOU** are the Whale who

ALWAYS wants **MORE**

But **WHAT** are you

really wanting it

FOR?"

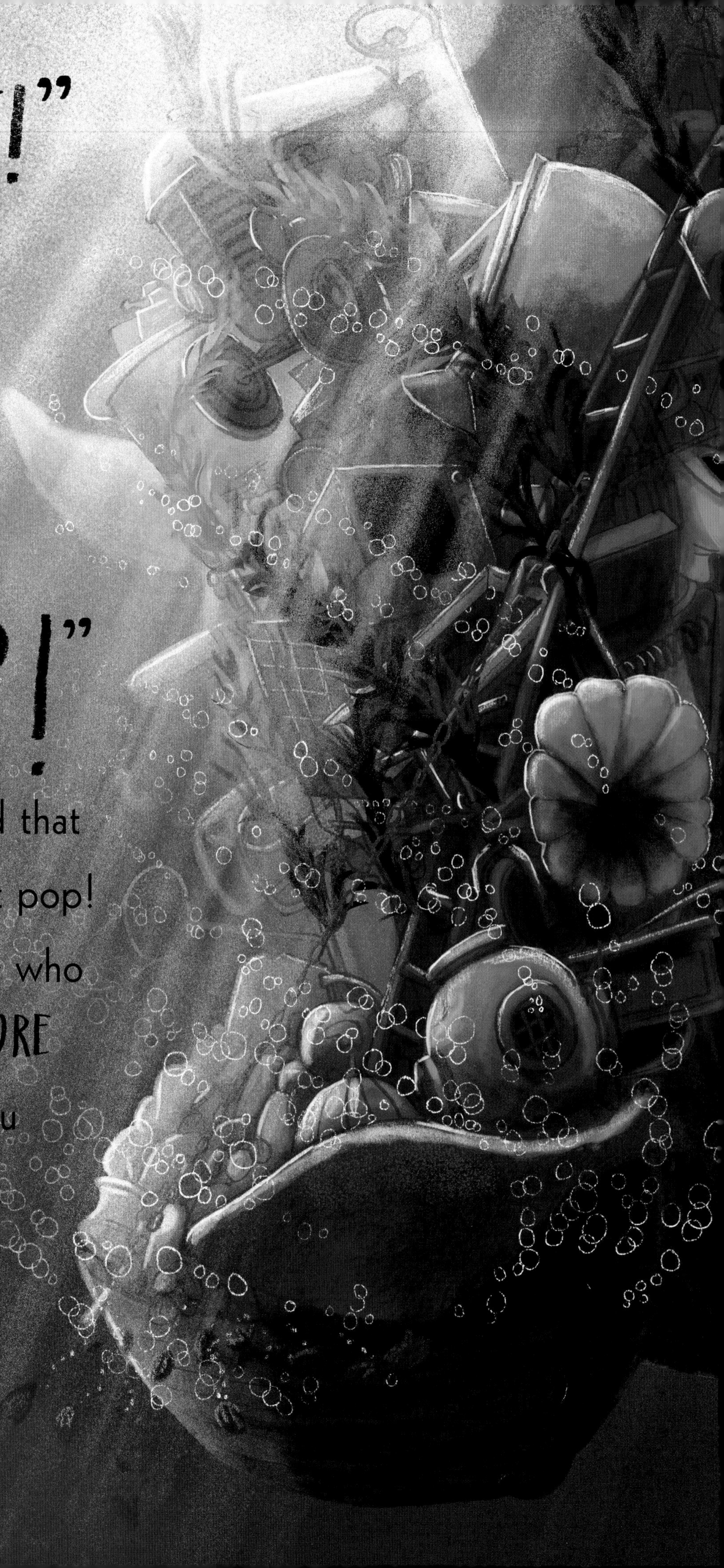

Well, Humphrey was
utterly taken aback.
This feisty young crab stopped
him still in his track!

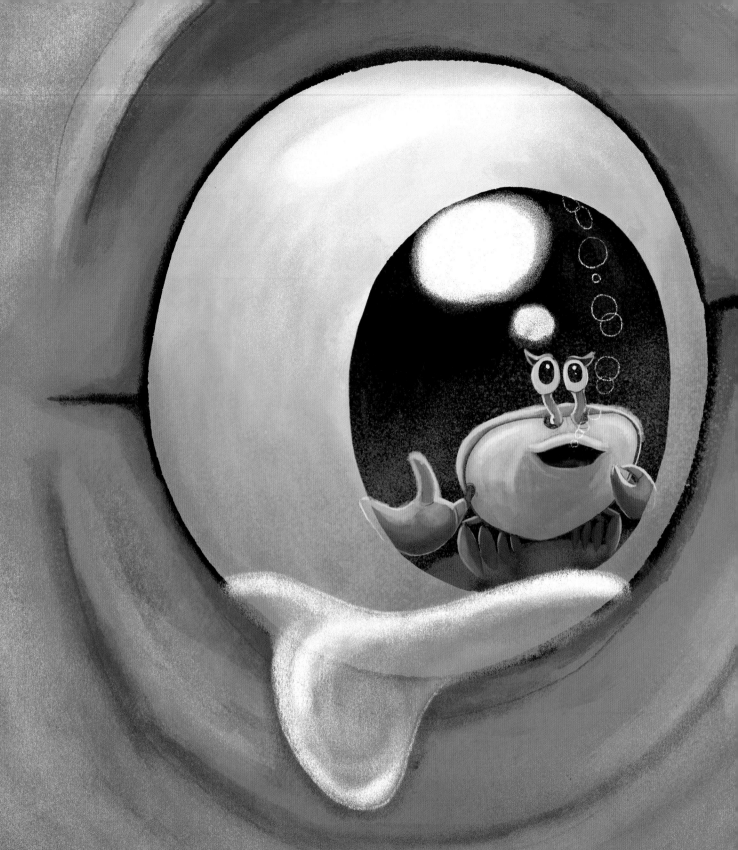

He thought very hard, for the first time in years,

As he gathered his voice, so he fought back some tears.

"I . . . don't . . . know," whispered Humphrey. "I think that my goal

Was to feel all filled-up and, well, happy and . . . WHOLE."

"You know," replied Crystal, "I think you might find
That happiness comes when you're CARING and KIND.
Perhaps . . ." she suggested, with one pincer uncurled,
"You might have a gift you could GIVE to the world?"

Humphrey, he hung on her every word,
And deep in his soul, a melody stirred.
He remembered a lullaby, taught by his mother,
Echoed through time from one whale to another.

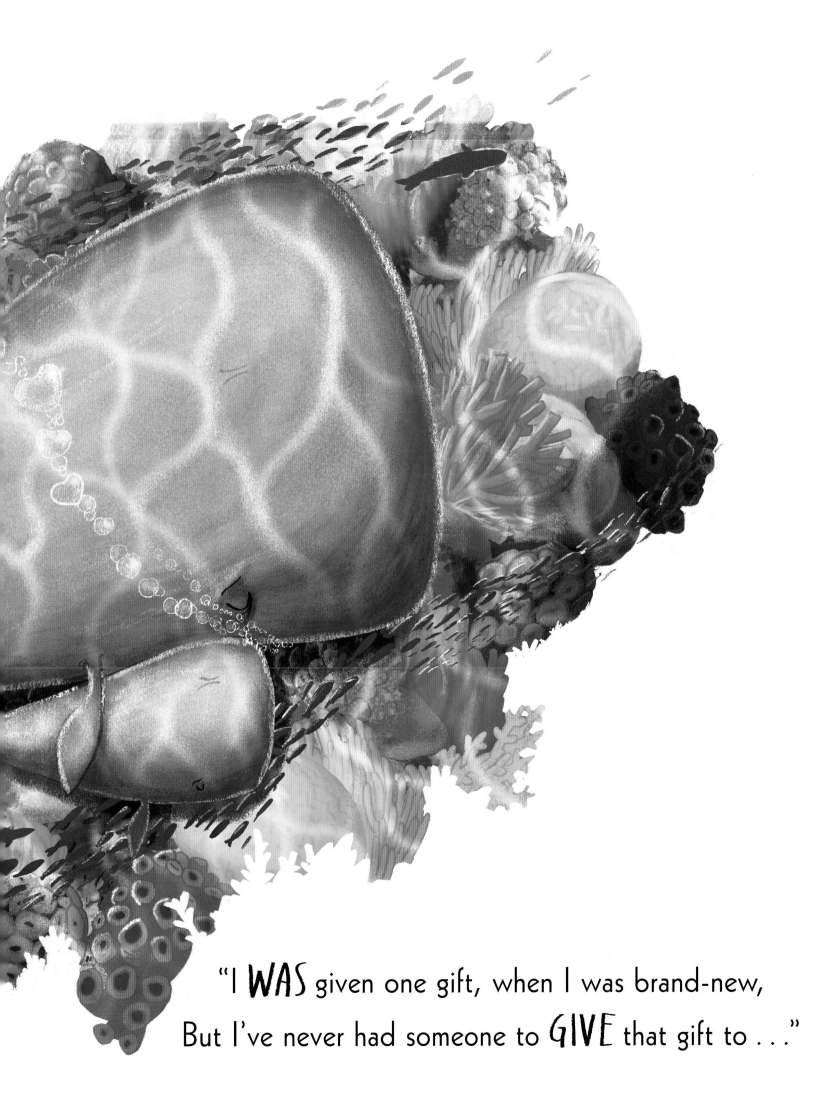

"I **WAS** given one gift, when I was brand-new,
But I've never had someone to **GIVE** that gift to . . ."

Then he opened his mouth, let go of his doubt . . .
And an achingly beautiful tune tumbled out.
The turtles, they circled, the dolphins were playing,
Even the seaweed was dancing and swaying!

And as harmony touched
every one who was there,
They remembered that balance
takes patience and care.

They'd been fighting
and poking and
griping so long,
They'd forgotten they
all sang the same

OCEAN SONG.

Humphrey, he knew then,
he wanted to stay,
As at last, all his
longings . . . they had
faded away.

From then, all was rhythm and peace on the reef.

For one clever young crab, it was quite a relief.

She befriended the whale, who perfected the knack

Of taking the time to GIVE some things back.

Yes, that whale stopped collecting

and made a great start

At doing the things that
FILLED UP his heart.

So perhaps true contentment,
is not about **STUFF...**

. . . Since we all need
SO LITTLE
to have quite enough.